B-I-N-G-O

Illustrated by Dorothy Stott

Published by Twin Sisters Productions
4710 Hudson Drive
Stow, OH 44224 USA
www.twinsisters.com

Executive Producers: Kim Mitzo Thompson, Karen Mitzo Hilderbrand
Music Arranged by Hal Wright

Made in Korea

ISBN: 978-159922-250-9

When you see  ,  , and  ,
clap and bark in place of the missing letters.

There was a farmer had a dog

and Bingo was his name-o.

B-I-N-G-O, B-I-N-G-O, B-I-N-G-O,

and Bingo was his name-o.

There was a farmer had a dog

and Bingo was his name-o.

 -I-N-G-O,

 -I-N-G-O,

 -I-N-G-O,

and Bingo was his name-o.

There was a farmer had a dog
and Bingo was his name-o.

- -N-G-O,

- -N-G-O,

- -N-G-O,

and Bingo was his name-o.

There was a farmer had a dog

and Bingo was his name-o.

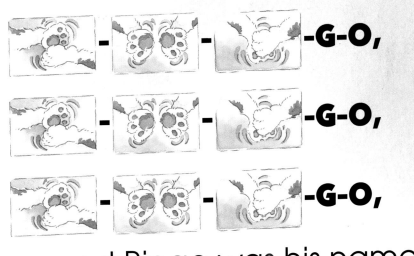 -G-O,

-G-O,

-G-O,

and Bingo was his name-o.

There was a farmer had a dog

and Bingo was his name-o.

and Bingo was his name-o.

There was a farmer had a dog

and Bingo was his name-o.

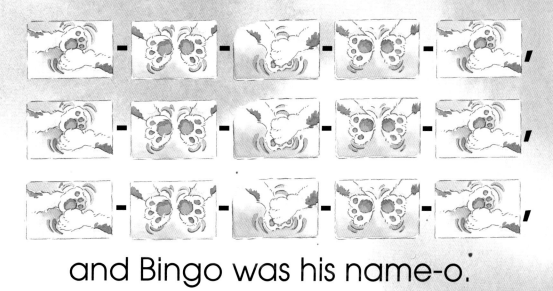

and Bingo was his name-o.

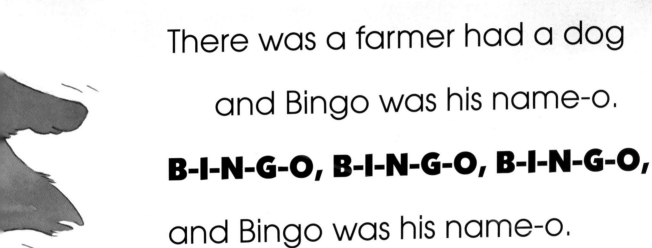

There was a farmer had a dog
and Bingo was his name-o.
B-I-N-G-O, B-I-N-G-O, B-I-N-G-O,
and Bingo was his name-o.

Bingo is the farmer's favorite pet. Draw your favorite pet.